Shoot a Hoop

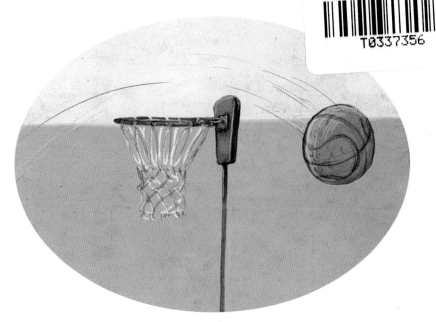

Written by Sasha Morton
Illustrated by Francesco Ghersina

Collins

Nick shoots a hoop.

His shot is too high.

Lee shoots a hoop.

Her shot is too short.

6

Lee is not sure.

She shoots in the air.

It is in the net!

10

Nick is not sure.

He shoots and dunks into the net!

13

In the net

too high

higher

too short

further

After reading

Letters and Sounds: Phase 3

Word count: 62

Focus phonemes: /ee/ /igh/ /oo/ /or/ /ur/ /air/ /ure/ /er/

Common exception words: into, the, he, she, me, you

Curriculum links: Understanding the World: People and communities

Early learning goals: Understanding: answer "how" and "why" questions about their experiences and in response to stories or events; Reading: children use phonic knowledge to decode regular words and read them aloud accurately, read some common irregular words, demonstrate understanding when talking with others about what they have read

Developing fluency

- Your child may enjoy hearing you read the book, modelling reading with expression.
- Ask your child if they would prefer to play the "role" of Lee or Nick. Look at pages 6 to 7. One of you should be Nick by reading his speech bubble in character. The other can be the "narrator", reading the text on page 7. Now do the same for pages 10 to 11, with one of you playing the part of Lee and the other the narrator.

Phonic practice

- Practise reading words with long vowel sounds together. Look at the word **shoots** on page 2. Sound talk and blend the letter sounds to model reading it to your child: sh/oo/t/s.
- Ask your child if they can see any other words on the page that include the "oo" grapheme. (*hoop*) Ask them to sound out and blend the letter sounds: h/oo/p.
- Now do the same with the word **high** on page 3: h/igh.

Extending vocabulary

- Read page 3 to your child. Ask them to point out the word that describes the type of shot, i.e. how the ball moves. (*high*)
- Now do the same using page 5. (*short*)
- Look at pages 14 to 15. Talk about all the words that describe different types of shots, using the pictures to help with the meaning. Now ask your child if they can think of any other words to describe shots. (*fast, slow, under, over*)